Note

Spanning several thousand years, from the ancient civilizations of Egypt and Assyria, to the classical eras of Greece and Rome, these illustrations offer a rich trove of full-color fashion history. Some 700 detailed, accurate renderings, each with a descriptive caption, depict modish ladies dressed in an enormous variety of costumes, from the linen skirts of ancient Egypt to the pallas of Greece, and the graceful togas of ancient Rome. Discover the sheer scope of this collection, which includes not only garments worn by slaves, workers, dancers, servants and other common people, but the clothing of queens, goddesses, and mythological figures as well. In addition to a broad range of gowns, tunics, cloaks, mantles, skirts, blouses, dresses, shawls, and other clothing developed over the centuries, you'll also find shoes, sandals, boots and other footwear worn by women in the lands of the Mediterranean and Near East. And, of course, no well-dressed lady of the ancient world would be complete without the proper headdress and hairstyle, along with decorative accents in the form of rings, bracelets, brooches, ornaments, earrings, necklaces, and more. All these costume elements are here, beautifully rendered and colored, and carefully reproduced from a rare French portfolio. Anyone interested in fashion or costume will want to study and savor this remarkable collection.

13·50

Wor
the
70

of
d

Dover Publications, Inc.
Mineola, New York

Bibliographical Note

This Dover edition, first published in 2005, is an original selection of plates from *The History of the Feminine Costume of the World, From the Year 5318 B.C. to Our Century,* published in two volumes by Foreign Publications, Inc., New York, 1926-27. The original text has been omitted; the French captions have been replaced by English translations.

DOVER *Pictorial Archive* SERIES

Library of Congress Cataloging-in-Publication Data

Giafferri, Paul Louis de, b. 1886.
    Women's costume of the ancient world / Paul Louis de Giafferri.—Dover ed.
        p. cm.
    Originally published: History of the feminine costume of the world, from the year 5318 B.C. to our century. Foreign Publications : New York, [1926–1927].
    Original text has been omitted; French captions have been replaced by English translations.
    ISBN 0-486-44527-5 (pbk.)
    1. Women's clothing—History. 2. Clothing and dress—History. I. Giafferri, Paul Louis de, b. 1886. History of the feminine costume of the world, from the year 5318 B.C. to our century. II. Title.

GT1720.G53 2005
391'.2—dc22

                                                                                    2005051793

Manufactured in the United States of America
Dover Publications, Inc., 31 East 2nd Street, Mineola, N.Y. 11501

Ancient Egyptian Costume

1. Ceremonial dress of Pharaoh's wife. Detail of the costume in the time of Ramses and Assurbanipal. Short waist-garment of pleated flaxen gauze, adorned behind with a jackal's tail and in front with a sort of stiff apron in gold and coloured enamels; long gown of fine linen with short sleeves, sharp pointed sandals; white cap striped with red and ornamented with the uræus.

2. Theban woman's dress in the time of Ramses and Assurbanipal. White linen pleated dress.

3. Interior bas-reliefs of a monument.

4. Flaxen gauze dress of Arboussemboul.

5. Cleopatra in divine parure, from the temple of Arthor Evergete in the isle of Philæ. Head-dress of braided tresses, perhaps a wig tied with a ribbon bearing the uræus, etc.

6. Anombreh, with consecrated colours and the ghost of the goddess (Great temple, Isle of Philæ). On the head is a sort of tuft of feathers.

7. Mouth : divine figure of Nubian origin.

8. White linen smock-frock, yellow belted.

9. Nubian head-dress.

10. On the banks of the Oronte. Coiffure ornamented with the uræus and inlaid with precious metals ; broad bandlets hang behind. Leather jerkin.

11. Pleated dress (flaxen).

12. Garment from an antique sculpture.

1. Irregular tunic finely pleated and edged with
   a high gold fringe; long sleeves fitting tight
   on the arm.
2. Fine flaxen tunic tightened with a belt round
   the waist (from masculine document).
3. Sky blue draped cloak bordered with gold,
   red and gold coiffure.

4. Royal costume in gold and colour, with the
   top of pleated flax galloon and coiffure of gold
   and blue plaited wool.
5. Long tunic made tight on the arms with bracelets (from masculine document).
6. Printed tunic, extremely tight, fastened together
   with braces.

7 and 9. Egyptian materials in various tints
   and embroideries.
8. Gown garnished with a pleated belt apron and
   a gold motif (masculine document).
10. Gown with double skirt, edged with coloured
   galloon; the grey galloon begins at the collar
   and shows on the naked bust.

N. B. — The above garments are common to both sexes but the women, kept in constant confinement, are less often figured.)

PLATE 2   ANCIENT EGYPTIAN

1. Queen's bracelet of massive gold formed of three parallel bands set with turquoises.
2. Queen Theki's gown, with green and light yellow stripes; green and white girdle, striped with red, tied in front. Fringe at bottom of gown.
3. Queen Taourra. Finely pleated striped gown, yellow belted. Head-dress with green and red feathers and blue veil within narrow red and gold circle.
4. Gown with big sleeves falling along the arms. White striped with blue. The large long girdle is tied in front. The hem of the gown is fringed. Bodice collar embroidered in several colours.

5. Gown (copied from a man's dress). Corselet with shoulder-straps. Belt with gold buckle. Gown striped with green and brown. Wrought metal bracelets.
6. Panel-border found during the Tut-Ankh-Amon excavations in a chest containing the royal robes.
7. Band terminating the panel of the back of Tut-Ankh-Amon's throne reproduced in embroidery.
8. Painting in a temple at Thebes. The gown is of a light transparent material, striped and crossed in front. Apron-girdle fastened in front.
9. Gold breast ornament found in the tomb of Tut-Ankh-Amon, gold, emerald, lapis-blue, obsidian.

10. Painting in an hypogea at Thebes. Gown beginning under breast and held on the shoulders with embroidered bands. Knotted girdle.
11. Gown copied from a man's dress. The tunic resembles the wings of a vulture. Pleated gown-bottom. Blue corselet checked with black and red shoulder-strips.
12. Woman's dress covering the whole chest, red.
13. Gown with broad coloured bands. The tunic is of light transparent material. A red and blue embroidered band forms the belt.
14. Gown from copied man's robe. Tortoiseshell corslet, striped tunic, bottom of the gown finely pleated.

1. Yellow cloak striped green and blue. Bright blue lining and yellow border; bow on shoulder.
2. Pink cloak edged with gold-yellow; white gown belted with blue. The neck-opening of the gown is round and gathered.
3. Gown with a blue yoke strewn with big spots; blue bands at the bottom with big spots, red stripes, and still lower, where the winding of the robe ends green band, white and red stripes.
4. Cuff embroidery, Nubian sleeve, lotus and ibis.
5. Gold head-dress with coiled green serpent, thick braids over the ears; behind, a blue and red flap. Bodice adorned on the neck with green, yellow and red embroidery, on light rust with dark spots.
6. White gown with red and blue bands; red and blue girdle; round-cut neck with yellow, green and blue bands.
7. Light yellow garment embroidered in darker tones. Blue necklace and bracelet.
8. Gown with high pleated flounce. Gown dark blue and the pleated flounce light blue. Yellow under-skirt.
9. Coiffure and collaret adorned with fringes.
10. Blue coiffure, yellow gown adorned with cunei-form embroidery. Blue girdle.
11. Arab dancing-girl. Blue bodice, yellow sleeve-bottom. First skirt green, second skirt yellow and yellow trousers.
12. Garment adorned with embroideries round the neck, yellow corslet, adorned with small coloured shells, bottom green with yellow stripes.

PLATE 4 ANCIENT EGYPTIAN

1. Egyptian woman's tunic, white with blue stripes, cobalt with carmine dots.
2. Bust garment : white lawn veil, yellow collaret, orange girdle, blue coiffure with carmine and yellow stripes, from the picture of Queen Nebts. 9th. Dynasty.
3. Egyptian dancer ; white lawn tunic, head-dress from a painting of Thebes. 5th. century BC.
4. Emblem taken from the temple of Beit-el-Ouali (Nubia) representing Ramses II threatening a prisoner. Blue attribute, vermilion red body, emerald-green wings.
5. Gown of yellow lawn, from funeral scenes in the painting at Thebes (Gournah temple).
6. Blue mitre. Ornamental flap Sienna brown, collaret, white lawn bodice, Comb with central ornament and lateral bands. From a masculine dress, bas-relief in the palace of Menephtha I at Karnac.
7. Egyptian queen's costume. from a painting at Thebes.
8. Blue and yellow coiffure, light brown and dark brown panther's skin, girdle and principal motif yellow ; side motifs red, carmine and blue. Bas-relief in the palace of Menephtha at Karnac. (From masculine dress.)
9. White tunic with carmine, emerald-green and light cadmium designs.
10. Dress material with carmine-red ground and green and light yellow designs. Light yellow collaret with red and green designs.
11. Red stuff with blue and yellow designs. Detail from bas-relief, picturing: Seti the First, father of Sesotris presented by Horus, the kite-headed god, to Osiris beside whom stands the goddess Hathor.
12. Waist-garment. Principal motif checked with blue, red, green, surrounded by yellow. Yellow motifs. Details from above bas-relief.
13. Bust-garment on cherry-red laquered lawn, yellow collaret with white, emerald and yellow motif. Blue girdle with yellow design. (Thebes, Medenet-Habou.)
14. Collaret forming sleeve, yellow with red design. Light-blue coiffure and gown. (Excavations in Nubia.)

1. Galloon embroidery, wavy braid (green, blue, red). Egyptian dress 3rd. to 13th. century.
2. Embroidery band, seyantich motif, blue and yellow.
3. Sleeve forming vulture-wings, from a bas-relief in the tomb of Souhem. Auditor of Justice of Amounof I leader of the XVIII Dynasty.
4. Sleeve from a bas-relief representing Schamthe. (Masculine document.)
5. Very short sleeve. Costume of Sevekoph.
6. Sleeve formed out of a beast's skin, funeral stele of the high-priest Pischarenptah.
7. Embroidery design formed of arabesques and intertwinings, Egyptian costume, 3rd. to 12th. century, 2nd. period.

8. Sleeves adorned with red embroideries.
9. Embroidery from a gown (neck and sleeves), Egypt between 3rd. and 12th. century.
10. Sleeve of light muslin, Thebes documents, collar entirely embroidered, red, green, yellow.
11. Embroidery on Egyptian gown 3rd. to 12th. century, 1st. period.
12. Very light muslin sleeve over an arm from bas-relief in Karnac palace. A curious fragment from a sculpture of Amounoph III.
13. Embroidery with narrow blue and orange galloon. Egyptian costume 3rd. to 12th. century.
14. Sleeve of stiff material forming part of the gown-top, from bas-reliefs destroyed by the last Kings of the 23rd. dynasty.

15. Embroidery of gown-top forming neck and sleeves. Egypt, 2nd. to 12th. century.
16. Very light veil of the gown forming sleeve, from a stele in the British Museum.
17. Light muslin garment, large sleeve.
18. Muslin sleeves starting from the collar, resembling the wings of a butterfly. Queen's dress.
19. Masculine document, sleeve fixed at the waist. From a detail in a bas-relief.
20. Embroidered medallion, blue, red and yellow. Egyptian costume, 3rd. to 12th. century.
21. Short indented sleeve, embellished with a green ornament hanging on the shoulder.
22. Short yellow veil sleeves, from a figure in a scene of offerings to the goddess Rabbon, Thebes.

PLATE 6   ANCIENT EGYPTIAN

1. Egyptian coiffure, old red and light blue, with torsades.
2. Very high-crowned hat, red ochre.
3. Egyptian coiffure, bright yellow and green, with wings.
4. Coiffure of Queen Ameritis (25th. dynasty), green-blue and brown.
5. Coiffure of King Akkouvaton (23rd. dynasty), blue and light yellow, mitre.
6. Brown Egyptian coiffure, edged with yellow and ornamented in red, green and blue.
7. Coiffure of the god Horus, with light blue and dark blue stripes, trimmed with yellow and red embroidery, called *claft*.
8. Coiffure of the goddess Ammion, brown with light yellow stripes, garnished with two yellow ears and surmounted with a huge ornamentation in the shape of a green dome.
9. Coiffure of Prince Mantouhichopchof (19th. dynasty), blue with yellow embroideries, adorned with a red ribbon. Collaret.
10. Top of coiffure of the goddess Isis, yellow and red.
11. Coiffure of Kombumbos, red, surmounted with a long ornamentation of ostrich feather in the shape of a pyramid, yellow, green, red.
12. Extract from a stele of Ramses IV " Maiamoum ", green coiffure, yellow collaret, red and green, in front of the sacred cobra.

1. Texture. Ochre background decorated with small columns, green and salmon-pink, violet-red.
2. Prisse d'Avesnes. Texture decorated with flowers and grapes, green-blue.
3. Prisse d'Avesnes. Brick ground, blue and cream decoration.
4. Prisse d'Avesnes. Yellow ochre ground, brick, blue, red, green, white decoration.

5. Textures. Green ground, blue and brick-yellow decoration.
6. Egyptian gown; the top, a sort of collar, blue, red and white decoration; the white gown is striped with red, green and yellow flaps, dots.
7. Green gown, black decoration, red, blue flaps, yellow girdle, green and blue material.
8. Band of stuff, violet ground, decoration yellow, red, white stripes.

9. Texture, violet ground, decoration yellow, red, blue stripes.
10. Texture, brick ground, decoration large green column with broad blue, green, brick foliage.
11. Pale blue texture, purple and yellow-white decoration.
12. Texture of varied hues, brick, green-pink, indigo blue and cream.
13. Gown covered with a sort of small cape, blue, purple, yellow, red-striped.

PLATE 8   ANCIENT EGYPTIAN

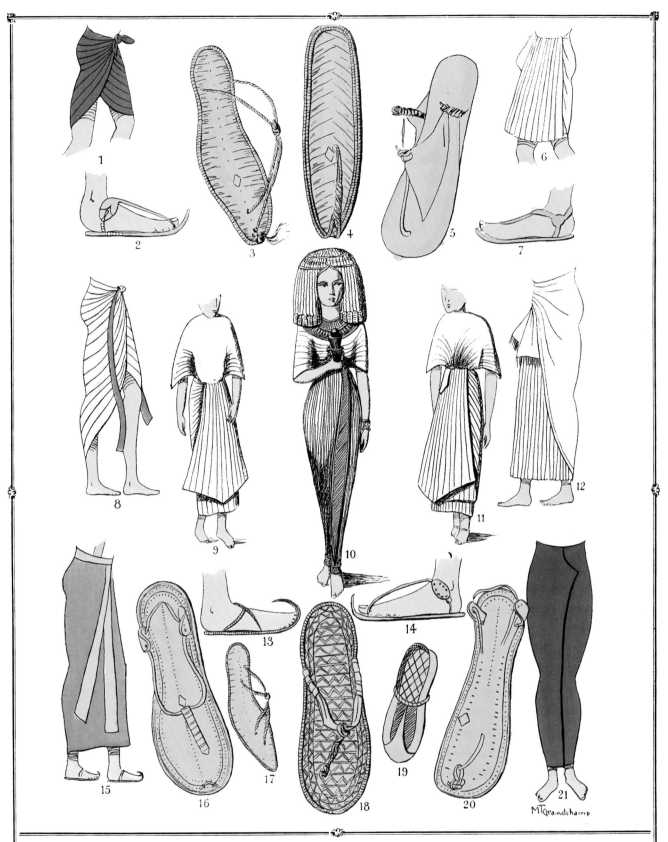

Ancient Egyptian costume. Figures 1 to 8 are about identical in style.

1. Winding arrangement of very fine material, varying in length, and fastened in front with a mere bow (short trousers).

2.3.4.5.7.13.14.16.17.18.19.20. Various types of rush sandals held on the foot with straps, one of which passes round the big toe.

6. This gown of fine linen is adorned in front with a very small apron.

This apron idea is often met with. The two statuettes 9 and 11 represent Egyptian deities dating from the end of the 18th. dynasty.

8. Draped skirt held up with a long cherry-coloured girdle with hanging flaps.

9. 10. 11. From the statuettes the dress of the new Empire can be reconstituted (Egyptian museum in Cairo). The biggest statuette is also an Egyptian deity from a wood carving about the end of the 18th. dynasty. The important head-dress of braided hair contrasts with the dainty silhouette; girdle with a long flap; heavy bracelets on the ankles and arms. The gown of very fine flax is pleated all over.

12. Long skirt entirely pleated in front, partly covered and fastened with a fringed belt.

15. Long and very tight green skirt, fastened in front; a yellow girdle fixes it round the waist and falls in two very long flaps.

21. Long blue skirt, very tight, formed of a winding wrap fastened in front.

1. Gold ring, seal.
2. Gold ring, chased and inlaid with 3 precious stones.
3. Ring, probably in bronze.
4. Gold ring, seal-ornament (cylinder), revolving.
5. Two-toned cornelian necklace.
6. Blue and red glass and cornelian.
7. Gold seal-rings.
8. 15. Woman's stiletto with damask blade.
9. Necklace of glass beads.
10. Necklace of notched red stones.
11. Bronze ring, scarab bezel.
12. Ring with scarabeous.

13. Necklace cornelian beads in different colours.
20. 21. 32. *The same.*
14. Ring adorned with a scarab.
16. Necklace, alternate cornelian and stones.
17. Scarab set as pendant.
18. Ring, silver seal, hieroglyphics.
19. Scarab ring, set on pivot.
22. Gold bracelet inlaid with green stones and engraved, hieroglyphic characters, gold serpents.
23. Scarab representing Ramses in the shape of a bird.
24. Cornelian and blue stone.
25. Leather dog's collar, the animals are cut out,

white glassware ; inside, leather of another colour.
26. Top of Egyptian princess's head-dress. Sort of halo of flowers which seem to be open and closed lotuses, in gold ; the main piece seems to reproduce the entrance of an Egyptian temple.
27. More modern figure showing the necklace of brown cornelian and the draped veil.
28. Ostrich feather and cobra Time of Ramses.
29. Seal.
30. Georgian slave. Puff ear-rings and broad pearl necklace.
31. Egyptian woman's pipe and tobacco-pouch of plaited straw.

PLATE 10   ANCIENT EGYPTIAN

Assyrian Costume

1. Pink gown with red embroidery ; neck-trimming yellow, like that of the gown.
2. Orange-yellow gown. Orange and green veil. Orange trimming in front of the gown. (Jeanne Dieulafoy. Excavations at Susa.)
3. Blue gown. Girdle with yellow and red embroideries. Green and red coiffure.
4. Green and yellow gown, with green ground and yellow ornaments ; red stripes in the lower part.
5. Green gown with pink and mauve stripes, brown belt, yellow band in the lower part and brown pleating. (From a statue.)
6. Excavations in the acropolis of Susa (plains of Chaldaea) by Dieulafoy. Yellow and violet gown. Orange veil. Light orange bodice and rest of the dress violet.
7. Excavations at Susa, by Jeanne Dieulafoy. Arab woman of the Cheik Hali tribe. Green veil and orange gown. Yellow band in the coiffure.
8. Capar of Loris workmen. Green gown adorned with orange bands on the sleeves; orange coiffure.
9. Blue gown trimmed with yellow bands round the neck, at the end of the sleeves, and at the bottom of the skirt, from Assyrian cylinders.
10. A. H. Layard, excavations. Blue coiffure ; top of gown pink and bottom blue, adorned with pink indentations.
11. Yellow gown with pink and yellow ornaments.
12. Statue of Nebo found at Nimrud. Blue gown adorned with embroidered cuneiform signs.

1   1. Yellow and blue whole costume from an enamel plate adorning the pediment of a town-gate.
    2. Dress sketched after a bas-relief in Khorsabad Palace.
    3. Chaldean woman, yellow flounced gown with red stripes.

    4. Gown from a bas-relief at Khorsabad.
    5. From an Assyrian sculpture, after a bas-relief.
    6. Assyrian Magician's gown.   This one is plaited at the collar.   Yellow border and sash.

    7. Whole costume from detail in enamelled wall.
    8. Woman's costume forming a drapery and fringes.
    9. Whole costume from bas-relief.   Draped skirt.
    10. From a bas-relief.

PLATE 12   ASSYRIAN

1. Gown taken from a Babylonian document, with yellow background and brown-red designs and fringes.
2. Gown forming a tunic, Naples yellow ground, green motif and golden-yellow fringes.
3. Tunic from a warrior's costume. Broad belt, fixing a round plate on the chest.
4. Richly-embroidered gown garnished with fringes forming a corselet.

N. B. Costumes common to both sexes.

5. Gown-top inspired by a masculine costume. Yellow bands crossing on the breast before fixing on a broad belt forming a corselet.
6. Pleated tunic from a masculine document. Wide bordered band.
7. On a Naples yellow tunic, a broad piece of fringed stuff, in the shape of a cloak, is folded on the shoulder.
8. Tunic in a sort a worsted with blue bands.

9. Fringed tunic fastened by a broad belt with wrought ornaments and little bands.
10. Large fringed gown with a flap falling on the shoulder
11. Assurbanipal's banquet. The queen, offering a libation, wears a pink embroidered tunic with golden-yellow fringes, falling over a blue gown. The sleeve is richly embroidered.

1   2   3   4   5   6

7   8   9   10   11 *Elvey*

PLATE 14   ASSYRIAN

1. Taken from a monument at Ninevah, bas-relief of Khorsabad palace, after a masculine document.   Yellow gown, green discs, red fringes.
2. Bas-relief in Khorsabad palace.   Green gown with yellow discs, red galloons, yellow fringes at the top, red ones at the bottom.
3. From masculine document.   Gown with fringes.
4. From masculine document.   The upper gar-

N. B. Costumes common to both sexes.

ment of Assyrian kings is also a shawl with fringes, often even draped more freely than the Chaldean shawl and simply flung over the left shoulder, also like the Greek cloak.
5. Costume from detail in enamelied wall.
6. Yellow dress with fringes, from masculine document.
7. Ninevah (Assyria).   Costume with broad blue and orange stripes.

8. Arab woman of Cheik Ali's tribe.
9. Mascate woman.   Green tunic with yellow discs and stripes.   Black trousers.   Sort of slit hood disclosing the eyes.
10. Woman's statue.   Sort of white shawl with yellow and red stripes.   Ochre gown, blue belt.
11. From Susian archer's costume.   Orange gown with blue discs, green and brown border.

1. Straight-cut gown with long coat and short sleeves.

2. Gown with a sort of draped pannier and double facing, embroidered with a galloon similar to the belt.

3. Gown entirely pleated, fastened at the side by a jewelry ball.

4. Long straight tunic, partly covered with a garment of gold embroidery.

5. Double-belted cassock over a pleated skirt with plain bands laid across.

6. Common woman's dress, draped in front and completed with a cap.

7. Gala dress with bolero of embroidered cameos and beaded hem.

8. Gown drawn in at the waist by a broad belt, with a facing and a band of ermine.

Gadin

1. From bas-relief in Khorsabad. Blue-grey sleeve, brown band forming fringe, small yellow and white band.
2. Small sleevelet forming old-pink petals.
3. 4. Scarf adorned with gold beads.
5. Sleeve of King Assurbanipal, ancient blue, brown, beige and white.
6. Sleeve of Assurbanipal's wife, blue garment spotted with brown, brown fringe, blue and red sleeve. Thoroughly genuine document.

7. Brown sleeve with small check-pattern.
8. From bas-relief in Khorsabad. White sleeve with orange and white band, bright yellow fringe.
9. Blue sleeve checked with brown. Gold bracelet.
10. Yellow sleeve with green and white band.
11. Orange-yellow sleeve, adorned with blue motifs.
12. Blue sleeve with small white check.
13. Blue sleeve with band of white embroidery.
14. Brown sleeve embroidered with blue. White band with similar blue embroidery.

15. Assyrian woman's green costume adorned with yellow and mauve bands.
16. Brown and blue sleeve.
17. Assyrian woman's yellow gown with bright blue band.
18. Brown sleeve.
19. Sleeve forming white petals.
20. Blue sleeve with brown bands, yellow motif.
21. Assyrian woman's costume with yellow and red tunic under white gown.

PLATE 16 ASSYRIAN

Bernard

1. Modest coiffure draped behind, of broad-checked material.
2. Woman's hair confined in a narrow band, the two fringed ends of which hang low down on one side. On the forehead, an embroidered and beaded motif adorns the band.
3. Small Chaldaean hat, with the crown covered by the tucked-up brim. This coiffure is adorned all over with similar motifs in the shapes of discs.
4. Woman's embroidered coiffure, tightly covering the top of the head and falling on one side like a veil.
5. High " hat-crown " worn by the Assyrians, with symmetrical trimming and cockade set in the centre, on the top of the hat.
6. Hat-shaped coiffure with scrolled trimming about the base and wreath of foliage in the upper part.
7. Assyrian King's coiffure in the shape of a helmet, with gold flower ; also worn by his spouse.
8. Wreath of leaves fixed by a double band round the head.
9. Cap with original helmet, trimmed in Assyrian fashion.
10. Pointed cap of stuff embroidered with galloons in several colours. Two side lappets are tucked down to protect the ears.
11. Royal tiara adorned with rosaces and geometrical lines. Two fringed flaps descend on the sides.

1. 3. Small ornamental motif forming galloon, brown and green ; 3 is yellow and blue with black central dots.

2. Picturesque fragment of Assyrian hunt. Decoration often found in embroideries or paintings on royal garments.

4. Pretty decorative motif for a gown-edge. The ground is pale blue, the motif a bird, etc., yellow and orange ornament.

5. Another embroidered gown-band (from mural painting in Nimrod's palace, blue ground yellow, red, sanguine, brown and white motif.

6. Embroidered motif for galloon on green ; the outline of the motif is yellow, the inside white. White chevron. Ground of decoration brown.

7. Small decorative galloon formed out of small white and buff palms on green support.

8. Central figure. A very beautiful Assyrian costume in all its richness. Document from a bas-relief in the palace of King Sargon at Khorsabad. The interesting cloak is all fringed with gold in front, disclosing a little gold-fringed skirt with the same ornamental motif. The upper part of the costumes is formed by winding fringes fastened with a galloon passing across the chest, partly covering the gown and hanging down the back, like a scarf.

9. Embroidered motif with beginning of a little edging in which we again find the winged bull so often met with in Assyrian decorations. Blue ground, yellow and red motif, white bull.

10. Embroidered gown-bottom, orange and green motif on white.

11. Fragment of white stuff with orange-brown and green motif.

12. Embroidered gown-bottom ; very rich and decorative ; this animal is quite typically Assyrian. (From Babylonian document.)

13. Ornamental motif with human figures and an orange and yellow rosace on white.

PLATE 18   ASSYRIAN

1. Venetian red strap (from Botta, designed by Flandin).
2. Sandal. Heel striped Venetian red and Sevres-blue. (Botta and Flandin, volume I, From a sculpture in Nineveh and a bas-relief in the Khorsa-bad palace.)
3. Sandal. Close-fitting heel, Sevres-blue, gold galloon and ring. Sevres-blue straps. Venetian red sole.
4. Sandal. Close-fitting heel and bright yellow strap, dotted with light green (After Victor Place).
5. Light yellow high boot, Venetian red laces and soles.

6. Venetian red shoe and laces (Botta and Flandin).
7. Woman of Mascate in Susiana. Black ash-green tunic, with Sevres blue design. hood, Venetian-red and black boots. (From documents found in the Susa Acropolis, Dieulafoy's excavations.)
8. Slave's dress. Long Sevres-blue smock, Malmaison-pink belt, bright yellow galloon at the bottom. Venetian-red fringes. Malmaison pink half-boots, black laces, brown and yellow leggings. (From excavations in Nineveh, by Victor Placet.)
9. Light blue-green half-boot, yellow galloon and

lace, white check legging, blue and yellow garter.
10. Malmaison-pink shoe. Black sole.
11. High Malmaison-pink boot. Black laces.
12. Very light emerald-green boot. Green laces.
13. Malmaison-pink gown-bottom. Embroideries in gold, Venetian red and emerald-green. Light yellow shoes, yellow laces.
14. Sevres-blue half-boot, Venetian red laces and galloons. Brown check legging, light yellow lace and garter.
15. Light yellow half-boot, check legging and brown laces.

1. Fly-flap, carved and coloured wooden handle. Coloured feathers.
2. Belt-pendant with gilt metal ornaments.
3. Assyrian princess's coiffure with principal motif forming a diadem. Very tall crown enriched with various ornaments : flowers, gold lattice-work. Ear-rings of chiselled gold.
4. 5. Irregular brown and yellow cornelian necklaces.
6. Gold bracelet of a single piece ending in animals' heads.
7. Diadem of stuff and gems. Chased gold ear-rings.

8. Gold bracelet with central ornament of different-coloured gems : rubies, sapphires, emeralds.
9. Diadem of precious metal forming large diminishing flowers. Chased gold ear-rings.
10. Gold ring with central ornament forming flowers in coloured stones.
11. Ring like the preceding one, but with the central ornament repeated all round the finger.
12. Noble lady's bag, sort of ornamented basket representing a typical Assyrian scene : angels gathering fruit.

13. Gold necklace in two parts, one tightly binding the neck and the other hanging lightly ; the former has tight and rigid links, the latter larger and more elastic links resembling chariot-wheels. Chased ear-rings.
14. 15. Chased gold ear-rings differently composed. The one (14) is a short, squat and rich model ; the other (15) a slender and very simple model, more elegantly chased.
16. Double gold bracelet, expandable.

PLATE 20   ASSYRIAN

Greek
Costume

1. Long amaranth garment reaching down to the legs over long white tunic. Front covered with broad gold plate engraved with lines and characters. Gold sandals.

2. Pomona's costume. Veil on head, draped in broad twist at waist, falling over white tunic. Diadem of gold apples.

3. Yellow flaxen tunic, draped and fixed on shoulder with strip and gold button.

4. Great piece of green stuff draped on shoulder over gown with wide mauve folds.

5. Blue mantle draped over pink gown.

6. Gown almost of Assyrian inspiration. Gold-embroidered green tunic. Red and gold sandals.

7. Dress of Panathanean woman in Parthenon. Broad-folded gown. Draped cloak flung over shoulder.

8. Blue gown clasped on shoulder and set over pale yellow flaxen tunic.

9. Gown open on left side showing the leg.

10. Black-bordered chlamys and scarf, tunic underneath, same border on long ample skirt.

11. 12. The woman sitting wears a red tunic covered with gold-blue mantle, yellow linen and wrought-metal embroidery. The other one has a yellow tunic and blue embroideries over white tunic. White band in hair.

1. Woman clad in short scapular over a loose-folded gown.

2. Costume composed of superposed red and green tunics over long yellow simple-folded skirt.

3. Greek girl in short-sleeved gown, draped waist. Garment and little scrolled socks.

4. Woman out of doors with mauve and green tiered tunic. Waving cloak.

5. Tunic draped on one shoulder, fixed by a cameo, stopping above the ankle.

6. Woman clad in light bloused gown with coquilles from shoulders downwards.

7. Long gown bound round the waist with gold tie.

8. Draped tunic fastened on the shoulders and waist, falling over the skirt in pretty draperies.

PLATE 22   GREEK

1. Short blousing green tunic over yellow skirt (Pompei excavations).
2. Fragment of painted vase figuring top of veil-tunic.
3. Great scarf set over gown with tunic (Pompei).
4. From masculine document. Greek soldier's tunic (Herculanum), also worn by women.
5. Yellow gown-top with great red bands, black girdle, from Isidi's temple at Pompei.
6. Great tunic with waist and sleeves reaching to the knees.
7. Yellow gown trimmed red and black, and red mantle trimmed black.
8. Blousing tunic tight under breast, partly covering the arm.
9. Tunic blousing at waist with a single semi-broad and semi-vague sleeve.
10. Yellow scarf over red gown.
11. Gown-top all draped entirely covering lower part. Tight gathered at back. From part of Panathanean procession in Athens Parthenon.
12. Scarf starting from shoulder, covering back and set again on shoulder.

ouaeaire.

1. Dress from Parthenon frieze " Procession of Panathanea ". Draped cobalt-blue tunic. Orange-yellow skirt.

2. Elegant Greek lady. Vermilion-red and blue coiffure. Cobalt-blue gown and chlamys. Gold yellow embroidery on chlamys.

3. Elegant Greek lady. Blue gown with golden-yellow border. Winding emerald-green scarf edged with black and white galloon.

4. Large draped mineral-violet cloak with narrow cherry-red madder band. White skirt bordered golden-yellow.

5. Elegant Greek lady. White attire fastened with orange string. Vermilion-red boots.

6. Elegant Greek lady. Cobalt-blue tunic edged red, cherry-red madder and embroidered black. Skirt with large pleats on cobalt-blue front. Orange band and black embroidery at bottom. Cherry-red madder scarf edged golden-yellow. Cobalt-blue and golden-yellow coiffure.

7. (Pompei buildings.) Terra-cotta statuettes.

Cherry red madder tunics. Light brown gown. Golden-yellow shoes.

8. Blue and dark green gown and tunic.

9. Mineral-violet mauve gown. Draped cobalt-blue scarf, gold fringes.

10. (Pompei buildings.) First tunic with large cobalt-blue sleeves. Second tunic draped, pink madder. Cobalt-blue skirt.

11. Cherry-red madder tunic, loosely bloused.

12. Mural paintings. A muse in emerald-green chlamys. Pink madder gown.

PLATE 24   GREEK

1. Draped skirt very low on the hips with coquille in front.
2. Gown-hem in very pale voile.
3. Veil-draped gown on a woman in Panathenæ frieze ; tied on side and falling in coquillé.
4. Gown of a Leda ; red with gold hem.
5. Dancing Bacchante's gown, in yellow voile adorned with light mineral blue.

6. "Greek", Fringe black motif on green.
7. Sitting woman with veil on hair. Red skirt with black band, draped tunic fastened on one shoulder and falling rather low on same-coloured gown.
8. Victory's dress, white vesture, violet-purple cloak.

9. Draped gown fastened on shoulders, back designs on hem.
10. Gown in voile, waist near its correct position. Green draped cloak, girdle very low.
11. From Naples museum. Half-naked young damsel.
12. Image of graceful Pompeian woman. Red ground.
13. A muse.

1. Sleeve in two parts fastened over the arm with row of yellow buttons.
2. Gown-top, cut low in point, leaving arms bare, but rather ample.
3. Gown-top forming simply an arch covering shoulders and half the arms.
4. Tunic with tucked cuffs edged with lace.
5. Striped sleeves, tucked cuffs edged with lace.
6. Dress-top, leaving one shoulder and breast almost bare, fastened on right shoulder with button.
7. Broad sleeve stopping at mid-arm.
8. Simple sleeve with tucked cuff edged with lace.

9. Little tunic with draped shoulder, big bow, mid-arm sleeve.
10. Very ample sleeve with motif at top, embroidered green.
11. Sleeves with godets stopping at mid-arm.
12. Very short sleeve.
13. Prettily draped sleeve, edged yellow, small tassels same tint.
14. Very simple arrangement with cuff at wrist.
15. Green muslin sleeve with folds shaped at mid-arm.
16. Sleeve with seam stopping at mid-arm and shaped.

17. Sleeve stopping at upper-arm with two rows of bicoloured motif.
18. Top for sleeveless gown. Ample girdle tied carelessly.
19. Statuette of Fortune. Ample gown-top with folds, violet motif at bottom.
20. Very beautiful shawl and drapery arrangement on one arm only.
21. Draped sleeve finishing in harmonious folds.
22. Tunic-top over arm but not round it.
23. This sleeve is beautifully ample and gracefully draped.

PLATE 26   GREEK

1. Plain draped stuff with darker border, tied on back-hair, hanging and hiding neck.

2. Bacchante's coiffure with small tresses tied up on top of head. Golden-yellow circle or bandlet on hairholds, ivy-leaves descending on each side.

3. From statuette. Coiffure of Greek girl wearing mitra.

4. From statuette. Coiffure figuring a cushion partly of plain ribbon and beaded stuff. Worn high over the forehead.

5. Phrygian cap of Greek prisoners with strings passing under chin. Also worn by women.

6. Short drapery of plain material, fixed behind, adorned with laurel on the sides.

7. Hat wholly covering head. Large brim tucked up in front ; free sides descending towards shoulders.

8. Small coiffure with narrow scrolled brim and two ribbons hanging together on each shoulder.

9. Woman's coiffure with ball-crown and tucked brim embroidered and edged. Coloured embroidery-stitches.

10. Diadem of goddess Artemis with engraved designs.

11. Large untrimmed hat.

1. Band from a painting in the Casa di Cecilio Giocondo, Pompei.
2. Band or galloon figuring stylized birds. Pompeian house.
3. Texture with geometrical designs.
4. Band of embroidery from Pompei.

5. Green, red and yellow embroidery. Pompei.
7. Stuff from hanging in Pompei.
8. Broad band embroidery, same place.
9. Band embroidered curves. Pompei.
10. Greek woman's gown with embroidery.
11. Band of embroidered ornaments from Pompei.
12. Curves embroidered on red. Pompei.

13. Band of embroidery. Pompei.
14. Band of embroidery. Pompei.
15. Broad embroidered band from Pompei.
16. Painted curves, black and yellow.
17. Herculanean painting representing Greek woman.

PLATE 28   GREEK

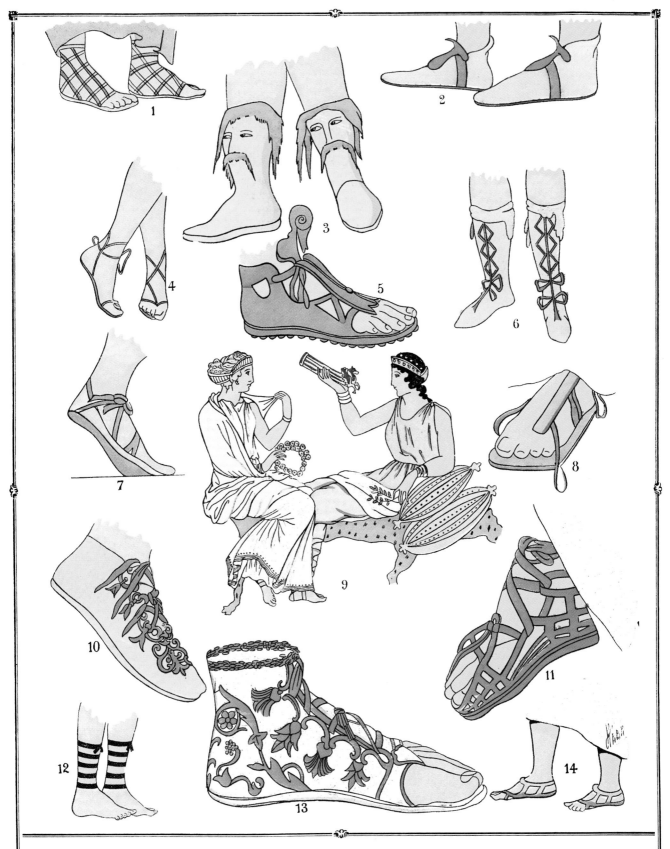

1. Sandal held by a quantity of straps, forming a squared pattern, found on a painting during the excavations at Herculaneum.

2. From the same source: footwear in soft leather held by a single strap.

3. High boots used during the conquest of Gaul; same source.

4. Sandals for feminine wear, held by straps gracefully disposed.

5. Very fine Greek sandals with perforated vamps, often studded with precious metal.

6. High boots worn by women. Taken from a statue of Diana at Herculaneum: yellow.

7. Thick soled sandals held by straps.

8. Sandals projecting from a peplus, square shaped, held by straps.

9. Scene from a Grecian meal. Indoors women often went barefooted.

10. Etruscan sandal: the uppers are beautifully worked.

11. Another Etruscan sandal, called of Sardanapolis, with highly wrought straps.

12. Lacing effect on legs, taken doubtless from the Etruscan crater of Vulci.

13. Beautiful Greek sandals, finely worked; repoussé leather, painted.

14. Sandals with open work uppers imitating straps; from a mural painting at Vulci, Etruria.

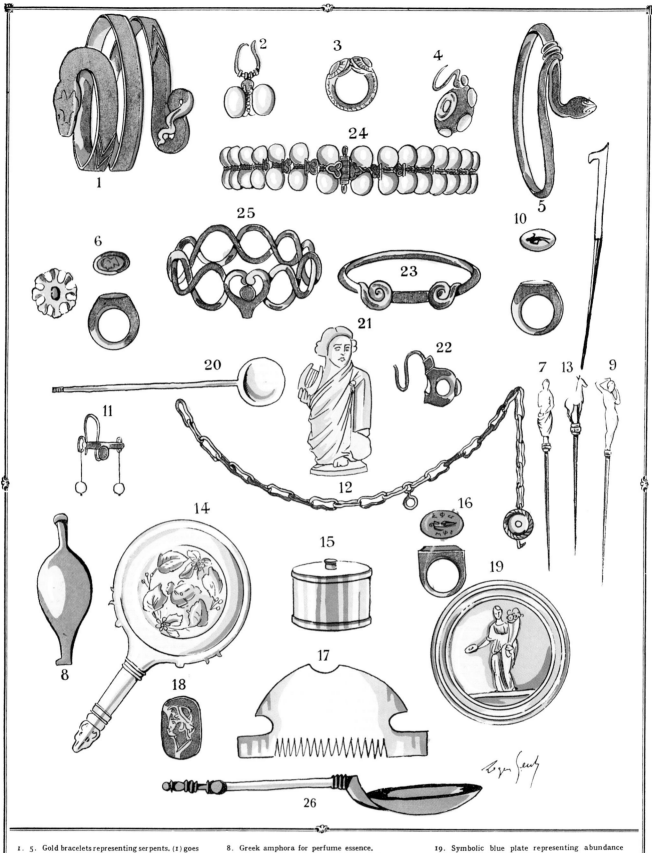

1 . 5. Gold bracelets representing serpents. (1) goes twice round the wrist, and (5) in which the tail winds round its neck, only once.

2. Earring in gold and two yellow pearls.

3. Ring : body and double head of serpent join to make bezel.

4. Gold earring, drilled in centre, enriched with emeralds.

6. Gold ring and red engraved stone.

7.9.13. Ivory pins on gold (7.9), representing woman of Greek statue type, (13) representing horse.

8. Greek amphora for perfume essence.

10.16. Gold ring, red engraved stone bezel.

11. Gold earring forming barrette with at each end thread bearing a pearl.

12. Gold link chain, end ornament round.

14. Back of looking glass in blue material, engraved leaf design.

15. Opaline vanity case, blue, red lined.

17. Blue comb decorated with yellow circles.

18. Gold medallion engraved classic Greek head.

19. Symbolic blue plate representing abundance offered to betrothed couples.

20. Perfume spoon, blue worked wood.

21. Perfume jar representing Greek personage.

22. Earring in gold with gold rosette.

23. Simple gold bracelet with two snail ornaments.

24. Bracelet or necklet in yellow stones with gold clasps. The stones are mounted in pairs.

25. Gold double intertwining bracelet, forming a heart in centre.

26. Perfume spoon in turned wood.

PLATE 30   GREEK

Roman
Costume

1. Toga richly embroidered and decorated, draped in folds over the shoulder, and falling in folds over the long dress.

2. Tunic and cloak held by a belt with long fringed ends.

3. Draped cloak scalloped and trimmed with gold braid.

4. Costume of an Etruscan lady richly decorated at the waist, sleeves and collar.

5. Roman lady dressed in a vast garment draped round the shoulders and taken in at the waist.

6. Fashionable Roman lady wearing a dress, with drapery covering the top, part of the dress and part of the skirt.

7. Roman lady wearing short-sleeved peplum.

8. Roman lady's cloak with the edges irregularly draped.

M.T Grandchamp

1. Roman toga, with which the head could be covered. It is red-bordered and held together with one hand.
2. Costume of a young girl, with green tunic and pale rose dress. According to designs discovered at Poitiers.
3. Costume of a Roman lady. The tunic is short and wide, held by a belt which fastens in front. The tunic is hung from the shoulders and shows the blue chemise. The dress is long.

4. Yellow dress with draped green scarf.
5. Draped robe in coloured rose, covering the head; caught up on one arm.
6. A Young Roman lady. The dress is pale green and high-waisted. Round her shoulders she is wearing a cloak.
7. Costume of a Vestal Virgin made of white veiling, with short-sleeves. She wears a purple mantle draped to cover one shoulder.
8. Costume of Flora. Mauve Penula. This gar-

ment is sleeveless and slashed at the sides for armholes, with another large opening for the head. The dress, white, is long and wide.
9. Costume of a Vestal Virgin in white veiling. The dress is bordered with a reddish purple braid. The sleeves are long and the cloak, thrown back over the shoulder, is purple in colour.
10. Young Roman girl. The tunic is short and caught in at the waist. The sleeves are short.

PLATE 32   ROMAN

1. Etruscan costume. White dress and blue tunic both trimmed with yellow.
2. Vestal Virgin dressed entirely in white veiling.
3. Priestess of Isis. The robe and tunic are white and the scarf mauve. The stars and other ornaments are silver.
4. Taken from a document written about men's attire.

5. Etruscan costume. Blue robe; yellow tunic falling irregularly.
6. Costume of Romulus. Note the Spolia opima also used by women.
7. Costume of a Roman dancer.
8. Large cloak thrown back over the shoulder. The sleeves are gathered.
9. Young lady wearing a white robe and a blue waistband, which resembles a cloak.

10. Tunic of a Roman gentleman. This type of tunic is also found in feminine attire.
11. Tunic of a Roman gentleman, trimmed with either large square or diamond-shaped scallops.
12. Costume of a Pompeian woman. A large bright green cloak with gold fringe and blue dress.

1. A large piece of material arranged over the head, twisted round the arm and falling to the hem of the robe.

2. Draped cloak passing over the shoulder and folded behind.

3. Draped cloak thrown back over the shoulder.

4. Cloak passing over one shoulder and held by drapery weighted with lead.

5. Short cloak rolled round the arm.

6. Cloak covering the head and rolled round the hips.

7. Cloak covering the head, rolled round the arm, so draped as to fall to the hem of the robe.

8. Garment thrown back over the shoulder; a beautiful effect of folds.

9. Short cloak fastened on the right side, falling lower behind than in front.

10. Short square garment thrown back over the shoulder.

PLATE 34   ROMAN

1. Costume of Roman dancer, veil winding round the body, leaving the hips bare. Light scarf.

2. Short frock starting from the belt, reaching down to mid-thigh.

3. Blood red costume leaving one shoulder bare, the other being covered by a tunic with wide sleeves.

4. Seated Roman patrician lady; wearing a draped gown and chlamys.

5. Greek costume consisting of a wide open cut bodice and a draped frock, all the frills being gathered in front. The back of the frock is very stretched and tight.

6. Greco-Roman drapery fastened to one shoulder and on the hips, bordered below by a fringe.

7. Dress of a Roman slave, draped around the naked torso.

8. Tunic fastened to the shoulders. Very high positioned waist, frock richly draped.

O. Macaire

PLATE 36 ROMAN

1. Bodice of red madder, trimmed with a band of embroidery forming a collar and running to the end of the sleeves. The band at the bottom is gold and the trimmings violet and red.

2. Robe of bright or dark caduminium. Embroidery of crimson lake. Scarf orient blue; belt green.

3. Dress sleeve coloured Etruscan rose. Skirt black.

4. Long tunic in blue celeste. Fringe variable, sometimes red. Waistcoat of reddish colour. Fair hair worn loose. The right hand holds a green veil. Blouse entirely closed at the back and held by a belt. Sleeves broad and shoes gold.

5. Rose coloured robe draped with a long cloak of sky blue.

6. Roman lady draped in a long tunic forming a veil over the head, and falling over a long dress. The whole toilette is white with blue and red stripes.

7. Garment closed at the shoulder. The sleeves are of muslin adorned by a series of folds at regular intervals. Dress of gold, cloak of violet.

8. Very short waistcoat open under the arms. Foundation of bright caduminium, blue stripes, girdle violet and the dress yellow.

9. Very short waistcoat entirely closed under the arms. Open over the shoulders with a flap hanging down the front. Foundation of gold material. Vermilion embroidery. Skirt ceramic blue. Embroideries Paris blue.

10. Very puffed sleeves in ceramic blue veiling. Dress foundation gold. Embroidery vermilion. Girdle reddish violet.

11. Short and very broad sleeves of sky blue; white braiding.

12. Robe draped over the left shoulder, broad sleeve, colour violet.

13. Very short waistcoat, foundation colour vermilion. Black embroideries. Collar, shoulder flap, and stripes at the hem gold black, embroidery, under the vest, in four parts gold; skirt orange.

14. Open sleeve of characteristically Roman type. Held together with a brooch. Dress orange yellow.

1. Greek headdress, amusing because of its cloak-shaped form, bright yellow.

2. Greco-Roman headdress in old rose from which hangs a veil.

3. Roman headdress remarkable by its originality, entirely plaited. A diadem of chiselled gold finished with a precious stone gives a generally enriching effect. A gold band rounds this sugar-loaf headdress.

4. Headdress composed of rose-wreaths.

5. Blue green headdress.

6. Roman headdress shewing the Focalia, a kind of band which the Roman ladies wore round the neck for the sake of warmth.

7. Wreath composing the headdress of a Roman lady.

8. Etruscan headdress consisting of a broad white veil lined with yellow and trimmed with a green band. The dress is cerise.

9. Roman headdress and garment. Purple veil, which falls in large points on to the shoulders. The dress, where the same embroideries

are repeated, is orange yellow. The shoes are vermilion trimmed with blue ribbons.

10. A Roman fiancée, wearing a large white cloak and a red veil.

11. White drapery, from which falls a brick-red band.

12. Headdress of a Roman lady, a kind of gold tiara encrusted with black pointed teeth.

13. This coiffure is attributed to a follower of Bacchus, it is recognisable by its characteristic features. These are: plaited hair, vine leaves and bunches of grapes.

1. Lady wearing a tunic over a sleeveless dress. A tight-fitting belt is worn round the waist.

2. Long straight robe the front of which is completely pleated. Front and hem of the skirt are embroidered.

3. Large Roman cloak trimmed with embroidered braid. On the background of the cloak are depicted the figures of athletes.

4. Roman lady wearing large hooded cloak covering the headdress. The wearer drapes the cloak and holds it up in front.

5. One-piece coloured fabric at the base of which a bright-coloured band supports circles and leaves embroidered with gold.

6. Band of plain material with chevrons embroidered at one extremity.

7. Roman cushion cover in drawn thread.

8. Etruscan fabric with pattern and triangles round the border.

9. Patterned dress material.

10. Design of a Roman fabric in bright colours on a dark background.

11. Braid embroidery.

12. Etruscan fabric in designs of two colours and flounced in another colour at the base.

PLATE 38   ROMAN

1. Footwear and the hem of the robe of a Roman dancer.
2. Footwear of a Roman lady in sea-blue bordered with red ochre.
3. Roman lady. Large violet shawl, yellow dress and blue footwear.
4. Footwear of the wife of Emperor Augustus, with gold straps.
5. Green prætorian footwear.
6. Vermilion footwear as worn by an Etruscan lady.

7. The footwear of a Roman lady in red felt or other fabric with two bands fastening under the instep.
8. Woman representing Venus. Sky blue dress; purple shawl; footwear of the same colour; fair hair.
9. Roman-Etruscan footwear in green with orange straps.
10. Braided feminine footwear in the time of Augustus.

11. Roman lady. Green dress, footwear of the same colour (for the theatre).
12. Sandals of the goddess Flora. The hem of the skirt is cream-coloured.
13. Footwear (with straps) of the wife of a Roman senator.
14. The yellow sandals worn by Patrician ladies.
15. Roman lady. Blue robe with a kind of large apron and red sandals like those worn by the Vestal Virgins.

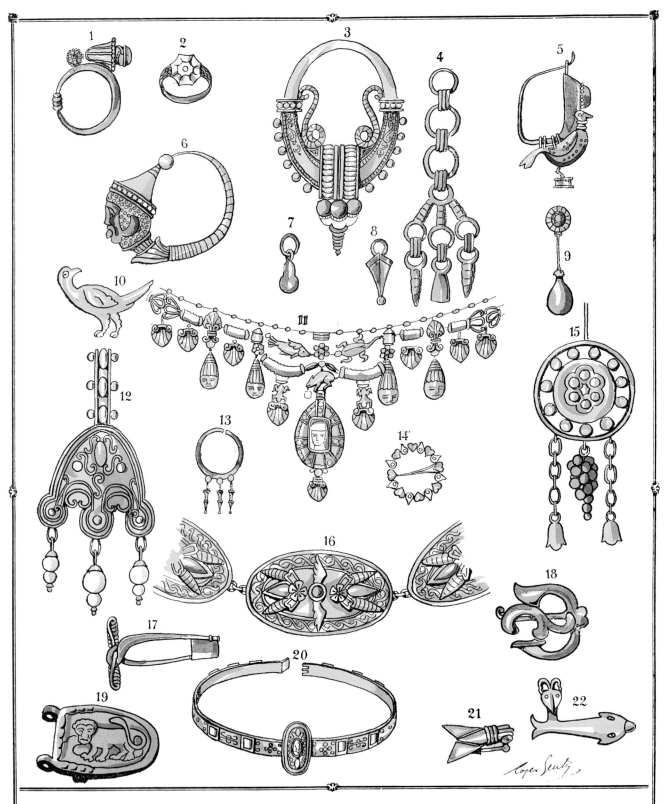

1. Golden earring (design tulip surrounded by small flowers).
2. Gold ring with green octagon stone.
3. Chased oval pendant; in the interior, wound gold thread; bellshaped at the bottom with a kind of ring. The whole ornamented and chased.
4. Chain pendant in bluish metal.
5. Gold ear pendant with red stone (design a bird with the body in red stone and the wings of gold).
6. Gold earring representing a laughing head wearing a pointed hat, and the tongue sticking out. Face in red stone, the rest in gold.
7. 8. Gold earring.

9. Gold earring. Centre stone bluish. Hanging stone pearshaped and red.
10. Brooch representing an eagle in repose.
11. Necklace made up of an agglomeration of designs. Flowers, animals and a human head interwoven by a green thread. The central motives are kinds of worked pendants : the centre is carved representing a head.
12. Pendant formed by a base-plate over which threads in relief form an interlaced pattern, towards the centre, picked out in precious stones.
13. Earrings, rings and ear-pendants.
14. Round heart-shaped brooch with a small stone picked in two designs.
15. Round openwork pendant with metal beads.

Chain pendant in the centre and a bunch of grapes.
16. Belt designed in a series of gold overlay plates with admirable graduated relief work; at the extremities, two sorts of bees with bodies in red stone : at the centre a blue stone with two wings.
17. Pin with a spring for security in fastening (probably the ancestor of our safety pin).
18. Brooch with a twisted design forming a decorative ornament.
19. Plate for a belt with a lion worked in relief.
20. A bracelet of simple outline, with a central scutcheon in which is a precious stone with engraving and chasing.
21. Brooches representing a bee.
22. A fish.

PLATE 40   ROMAN

Greco-Roman Costume

1. Greek citharoedes or women playing the citha-
   ra. Long flowery gown denoting a courtesan.
2. White gown, yellow drapery.
3. Long gold-embroidered tunic (Hamilton).
4. Long gown, gold border.
5. Long gown and tunic, gold border.

6. Long gown and tunic, gold embroidery.
7. Fashionable Greek lady. Long gown forming
   panniers on hips. Painted black stripes on
   white.
8. Long tunic draped on shoulder. Gold embroidery.

9. Short gold-embroidered tunic over long pink
   gown.
10. Long blue gown, orange veil.
11. Sort of *palla* fixed on shoulders and hanging
    in unequal points.

1. Gold-yellow gown. In lower part, cherry-red madder embroidered band. Wing-shaped sleeve and scapular, ceramic-green, embroidered cherry-red madder.
2. Emerald-green gown, striped black, neck and bottom embroidered gold-yellow. Sleeves forming long wings, ceramic-blue, edged cherry-red madder.
3. Great chlamys draped on shoulder, emerald-

green. Vermilion-red gown. Cobalt-blue coiffure.
4. Etruscan red gown. Black embroideries.
5. Etruscan pink gown. Black embroideries. Etruscan pink coiffure. Black embroideries.
6. Gold-yellow gown. Cobalt-blue cloak folded on legs. Gold-yellow coiffure.
7. Etruscan pink gown open in front, galloon embroidered cherry-red madder and white.

8. Metal violet tunic. Emerald-green gown. Green and gold coiffure.
9. Etruscan red gown. White fretwork in lower part. Black and gold embroideries. Red, black and gold cuirasse.
10. Gilt pink madder gown. Gold-yellow draped scarf. Gold coiffure.
11. Cobalt blue draped material, embroidered black and gold.

PLATE 42   GRECO-ROMAN

1. Short ample tunic, one side forming scarf, pink, over yellow gown. Collar edged with amaranth galloon.
2. Gown tight at waist and amply blousing. Draped on shoulders and fastened with two gold clasps.
3. Over a long yellow tunic, tightened mid-thighs and dropping blouse-wise is draped a white habit tight at waist, covering shoulder and hanging behind in a broad flap.
4. Little tunic, tight at waist and held on shoulders with two gold clasps, over long pale pink tunic.
5. Short tunic draped on shoulder. Very ample gown clasped on thigh which it shows. The whole is Etruscan red.
6. Etruscan red gown. Draped bodice falling in broad fold over gown.
7. Girdle-corset. Bandeau.
8. Etruscan red tunic with black designs. Similar scarf, bestarred.
9. Emerald-green short-sleeved habit, folded and draped on hips.
10. Gown with green tunic held on shoulders with two gold clasps. Yellow girdle, veil and scarf. Tunic made heavier in front with a sort of gold ball.
11. Etruscan red gown tightened at waist with narrow tied girdle. Black designs.

1. Long gown, yellow shawl of a dancer carrying a basket. A crown of vine leaves clasps her hair; her shoes have yellow ribbons.

2. Leto listening to the zither of Apollo, from an amphora (red on black background), excavated at Vulci, near Rome (Etruria).

3. Greco-Roman woman in draped cloak.

4. Large Etruscan cloak with borders.

5. Etruscan mantled shawl with borders.

6. Cloak with high borders.

7. Etruscan gown overlaid with a pastel tunic.

8. Pleated sleeved gown, hooded cloak.

9. A Greco-Roman woman after a fresco at Herculaneum.

10. Etruscan tunic and headdress, orange with black borders. (Almost all our Etruscan illustrations are taken from excavations at Vulci or Volterra, not far from Rome.)

PLATE 44   GRECO-ROMAN

1. Very light yellow gown with blue bands. Red cloak, black bands.
2. Gown folded in front, with, over it, the basque of a draped tunic.
3. Yellow gown with superposed tunic arrangement in other colours.
4. Gown with two bands of embroidery. Pleated tunic shorter in front.

5. Light green gown strewn with designs, violet cloak with contrasting coloured bands.
6. Cloak with flap hanging in folds, over very dark gown.
7. Antique gown from terra-cotta figure in a 5th. century tomb. Excavations in Delphes island.
8. Dancer's gown in light muslin with red band, fastened at waist.
9. Pipe-player at table, gown entirely closed.

10. Gown with superposed arrangement, heavily draped.
11. Gown uncovering one shoulder, cloak embroidered at bottom.
12. Dancer at a meal. Veiling arrangement. Very loose gown and cloak forming pretty folds.
13. Dancer's muslin gown, scarf forming flounces.
14. Gown with sleeves. Cloak entirely draped, embroidered at bottom.

1. Drapery formed by chlamys, low neck, crossed light yellow. Drapery border embroidered black on blue.
2. Pleated tunic forming coquillé, elbow-sleeve, very wide at top, small flounce on neck passing over one arm.
3. Drapery fastened on right shoulder and hanging in yellow pleated point.
4. Red tunic. Gold edging on collar and sleeves, veil-pleated front. Scarf to match.
5. Little sleeves, gathered tight, fastened over the arm, bright blue. Darker tunic edged with black galloons.

6. Costume of Minerva witnessing Theseus' fight with bull. Long pleated tunic down to the feet. Cloak on shoulder showing little sleeves.
7. Woman in broad-designed gown with black fringe. Long loose sleeve with same motifs as gown. One hand holds a fan; supports herself with the other.
8. Artemis listening to a friend. Pleated gown covered with shorter tunic also pleated in front. A second tunic embroidered with red galloon ends in pleated points.
9. Tunic with round-cut top fastened on shoulders and partly covering the arm.

10. Sleeveless tunic with narrow belt round waist; very ample bottom forming big godets edged with black galloon.
11. Tunic-top, in voile, entirely pleated, fastened on shoulders and arms with fibulæ.
12. Rather long pleated tunic, covered with shorter one also pleated, fastened on shoulder with fibulæ.
13. Elegant drapery formed by chlamys, covering arms.
14. Little bodice entirely pleated fastened over the arm.

PLATE 46   GRECO-ROMAN

1. Etruscan lady's coiffure, orange-yellow and black.
2. Coiffure of blond Etruscan lady.
3. Helmet with gold wings.
4. Etruscan lady's coiffure with blue roll and yellow embroideries.

5. Green coiffure with yellow motifs.
6. Gold crown-coiffure adorned with precious stones, white veil.
7. Ancient red and black coiffure.
8. Coiffure of young brunette with yellow mantilla.
9. Greco-Roman coiffure, little yellow, orange and brown hat.

10. Dull pink coiffure. Brown and blue garment.
11. Dull red coiffure and black embroideries.
12. Woman with gold net over blond hair. Gold ear-rings.
13. Etruscan red and black coiffure.

1. Woman sitting. Etruscan pink gown.

2. Light blue draped gown. Pompei, Temple of Fortune.

3. Greco-Roman dancer. Head and arm covered with long drapery. Transparent yellow habit. White pattens on feet. Bacchante.

4. Greek antiquity. Tanagra.

5. Greco-Roman. Eastern Greek women, one with face slightly veiled.

6. Smart low-cut top.

7. Draped sleeveless chlamys.

8. Delightful robe, long sleeves decorated in embroidered material.

9. Draped gown and pleated undergown, the whole light yellow.

10. Etruscan costume. Blue gown with gold fringe and embroidery.

11. From sculpture by Phidias. Draped skirt of Greco-Roman girl (Venice).

12. Pompei. Etruscan pink draped gown, blue pleated skirt.

PLATE 48   GRECO-ROMAN

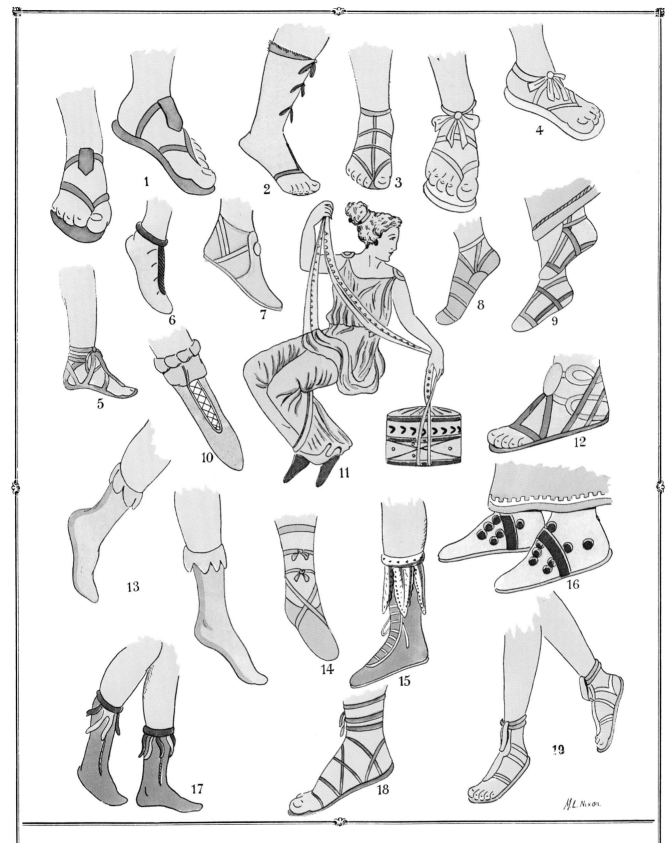

1. Greek shoe in brown leather, with green straps around the ankle.
2. High boot with scalloped lining.
3. Shoe with stap crossing on top of foot, double knot on ankle.
4. Sandal with strap over toes and heel, big knot covering top of foot.
5. Sandal with intercaled straps and leather tongue falling onto the top of the foot.
6. High boot rolled at top, laced in front.

7. Sandal with high uppers and tongue, adorned with metal ball and gilt straps.
8. Shoe with many straps.
9. Sandal held by transverse and horizontal straps.
10. Sandal with criss-cross straps held at the ankle by a ribbon.
11. Greek woman lifting a clothes-chest by a ribbon. She wears a rose tunic with galloons.
12. Shoes with elliptical straps.
13. Soft, seamless boot, pulled on like a stocking.

14. Sandal held by long straps winding round the leg.
15. High boot, laced in front, leaving the toes bare. Fur lining.
16. Embroidered leather shoe.
17. Shoe made up of crossed straps encircling the ankle; crinkled lining.
18. Sandal held by many straps.
19. Shoes with straps passing under a tongue that protects the ankle.

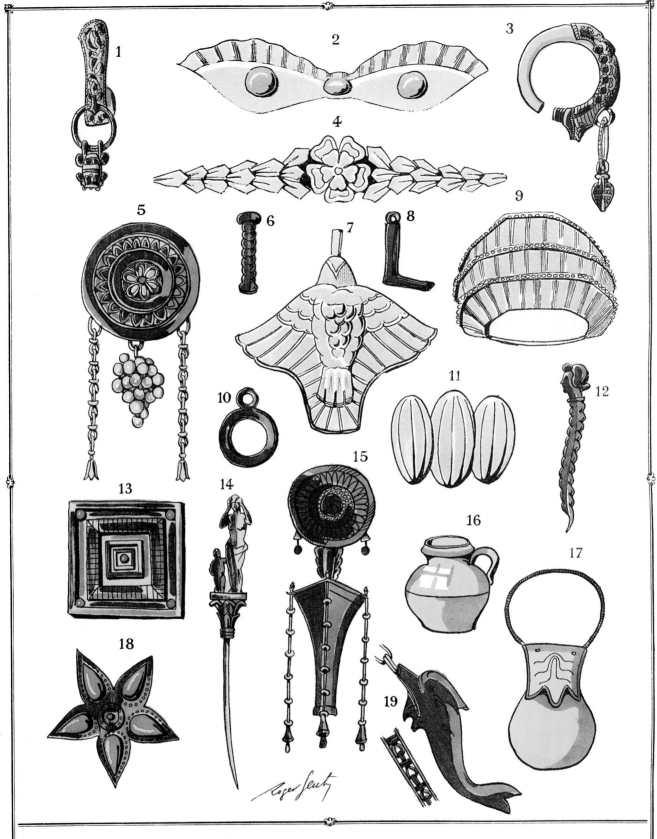

1. Sort of gilt and engraved pendant with ring upholding a vase-shaped motif.
2. Brooch figuring two wide-open wings with three big coloured stones.
3. Gold bracelet with vase-shaped pendant.
4. Sort of diadem. Central flower with wreath of leaves on each side.
5. Engraved rosace. In the centre, a flower inset with pearls. Chain-pendants on both sides and central pendant a bunch of grapes.

6. 8. 9. 10. Sorts of little pendants twisted, L shaped and circular, possibly amulets.
7. Metal pendant figuring a stylized bird with outspread wings.
11. Probably belt-clasp. Three olives in a row.
12. Pin with woman's head, twisted body.
13. Metal plate, square embossed ornament in the four corners and middle. Red stones.
14. Gold pin representing Greek statue, base shaped like Corinthian chapiter.

15. Fendant ; central rosace gilt and carved metal, continued in widening stem with three chain-pendants in angles.
16. Small glass jar for manicuring.
17. Bag-shaped paint-case.
18. Star-shaped brooch with five big coloured stones.
19. Detail of chain-bracelet. Fastening figuring two fish face to face, Christian Era.

PLATE 50   GRECO-ROMAN